F.R.E.E. YOUR MIND GUIDEBOOK

F.R.E.E. YOUR MIND GUIDEBOOK

Become a Better You

Published in New York, New York, by Aitia Press, a branded imprint of Morgan James Publishing. Morgan James is a trademark of Morgan James, LLC. www.aitiapress.com

Created by: Co-Founders Prime Hall, Don Tran

ISBN 9781631953217 paperback
ISBN 9781632953224 eBook
ISBN 9781632953231 audio
Library of Congress Control Number: 2020945896

Cover and Interior Design by:
Brooke Burns

Edited by:
Manuel Colon-Perez

Photos by:
Colton Tisch

Morgan James is a proud partner of Habitat for Humanity Peninsula and Greater Williamsburg. Partners in building since 2006.

Get involved today! Visit
MorganJamesPublishing.com/giving-back

F.R.E.E. YOUR MIND GUIDEBOOK

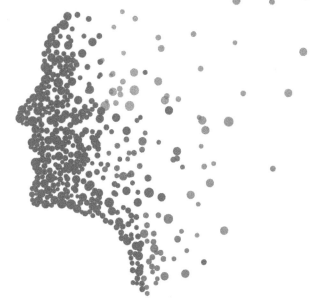

BECOME A BETTER YOU
An Operating System Created by Marine Raiders
for a Warrior Class of People

PRIME HALL & DON TRAN

AITIA PRESS • NEW YORK

TESTIMONIALS

"Prime has created a fundamental key and a high-level training system that integrates perfectly into my MMA training regimen. I could not ask for a higher quality of mental fortitude, breathing control and overall maximum lung capacity upskill, which is paramount in the fighting arena. I am grateful to be indoctrinated into a world-class initiative that is suitable to fulfill all athletic roles or tasks at a high caliber."

- DOMINICK CRUZ, UFC 3X CHAMPION

"This program is so unique to myself and being an NFL athlete. Every time I participate in the program, I could see humongous strides from the time before. Prime's breathing techniques helped to succeed underwater and translated to the football field. It taught me to remain calm under a lot of pressure. That's the type of activities you need to perform at your highest level. This program is the standard!"

- MICAH HYDE, NFL SAFETY BUFFALO BILLS

"The F.R.E.E. Your Mind training has impacted all aspects of my life from everyday events to competing at the highest levels. Out in the water I find myself a lot more calm and find it easier to stay relaxed in different situations. It also takes a lot of the pressure away and let's you work at your best level."

- COLE HOUSHMAND, PROFESSIONAL SURFER

"I'm very excited about the Underwater Torpedo League Program. Aquatic sports are among the most inclusive and healthiest activities possible. Prime's vision of an athletic yet safe aquatic competition has the potential to one day be an Olympic sport!"

- COACH DAVID MARSH, USA OLYMPIC SWIMMING COACH

FOREWORD

Mental fortitude is the tree of your life. Everything starts in the roots and soil. Like a tree, the quality and what you feed the soil will decide what branches grow and the fruit it produces. When we have a core of healthy and positive self-talk, our tree produces vibrant fruit. Competitive elite athletes seem unique in that they have a genetic advantage when, in reality, much of their success stems from healthy self-talk. Great athletes don't compete against others but rather (the best version of themselves). All of this sounds easy in theory but, being able to identify patterns of negative self-talk that are being fed to the soil of your being is difficult. Changing what feeds the soil of your tree of life will be difficult, but it is possible, and we get there by recognizing and changing our patterns of thinking. Just like a diseased or under-nurtured plant can be brought back to life, so can a weak mind in need of mental fortitude.

The concept of F.R.E.E. has been a game changer for my mental fortitude both within training and my personal life. Focus for me has made me more mindful of my life. I have a better perspective of what I want to achieve within training. In my personal life I am able to make goal focused decisions. Relaxation has helped me destress during difficult moments of training. To remember what I am focusing my attention on and to keep my sights on those goals. Economy of motion doesn't just apply in swimming. Economy of motion applies in that I've cut away unnecessary drag and clutter that weighs on me to help maximize my life. Efficient breathing has helped significantly in training. I'm able to relax my breathing and get more out of training because of it. During stressful situations during my personal life I'll utilize box breathing to calm down.

Leave your fears and expectations at the door.
Dive deep to new possibilities.

THE TREE OF LIFE

- **LIZ CARMOUCHE,** Professional Bantamweight MMA Fighter ranked #4 in the world

TABLE OF CONTENTS

INTRODUCTION TO THE F.R.E.E. YOUR MIND GUIDEBOOK AND OPERATING SYSTEM

The F.R.E.E. Your Mind Workbook was created by former Special Operations Marine Raiders Prime Hall and Don Tran. The program has been successfully utilized by former and current US Military Special Operations, Professional MMA Fighters, Olympic Athletes/Coaches, NFL Players, Pro Surfers, High Level Business Executives and more to break through "glass ceilings" and unlock their highest states of performance.

WHAT TO EXPECT?

The F.R.E.E Your Mind Workbook is an interactive, step-by-step workbook that makes the growth mindset a part of every day, every interaction, and every plan.
Designed for the busy individual, this workbook is filled with self reflective prompts, critical thinking exercises, and so much more. It includes space to:

- Reflect Throughout your Week
- Strategize Meaningful Discussion
- Exercise Mental Focus
- Practice Self-Talk and Mindset Language
- Set Achievable Goals
- Explore Your Successes and Failures

There are no exams or tests. There is no right or wrong way to use this guide.

THE MONTH-LONG GUIDEBOOK IS BROKEN INTO 4 WEEKS:
1. Assessment / Crawl Phase
2. Walk Phase
3. Run Phase
4. Fly Phase

Within Each Week, The Reflection Will Be Focused On Four Operating Principles:
1. Focus
2. Relaxation
3. Economy of Motion
4. Efficient Breathing

This principles and phased approach are used to maximize efficiency, create better habits, and reduce drag throughout your weeks and your life thereafter.

The purpose of this workbook is to show you (the User), the power of mindset in achieving your goals.

In this workbook, we show how life successes in business, work, sports, art, relationships, and almost every other human aspiration can drastically improve with self-talk and how we perceive our own talents and abilities.

People with a fixed mindset believe that their basic abilities, intelligence, and talents are fixed traits. In a growth mindset however, people understand that their abilities and intelligence continue to develop with discipline, effort, continued learning and persistence.

INTRODUCTION TO THE F.R.E.E. YOUR MIND GUIDEBOOK AND OPERATING SYSTEM

individuals with a fixed mindset are less likely to thrive than those with a growth mindset. Mindset reveals how we as great leaders, parents, managers, teachers and athletes, can utilize a growth mindset to develop outstanding accomplishments, not only for ourselves but for those around us.

> "Those who think they can and those who think they can't
> are both usually right."
> - Confucius

What is F.R.E.E.?

Success and happiness are no accident. Living a fulfilling life will not come by luck or chance, but by understanding who you are, what you are capable of, and how to apply your skills to achieve your goals.

The acronym **F.R.E.E.** stands for the operating system based on four principles of: Focus, Relaxation, Economy of Motion, and Efficient Breathing. F.R.E.E was developed to offer guidelines and key aspects to focus on to achieve that fulfilled, successful, and happy life. When all the principles are applied at a certain level, we can enter into a "flow state;" e.g. where things are working for us in full economy of motion, we "declutter" our mind and focus on what brings us closer to our goals and strategic purpose in life.

Mental Focus:

Focus is the ability to concentrate on the present and the task at hand. In order to fully maintain focus on one thing, you must inherently ignore distractions. Distractions come from external sources such as other tasks, people, or things. They also manifest through negative self-talk, bad memories and thoughts; or emotions such as fear, pain, or lust. In order to achieve peak performance and productivity, focus is key. Being able to say "no" to every other option unlocks your ability to accomplish the one important thing that is left.

Now, how do we focus better? Below are tools to improve focus and concentration:

Manage your energy, not your time: If a task requires your undivided attention, schedule a time when you have the most energy to focus according to your circadian rhythm. For example, if you have more creative energy in the afternoon, save your creative tasks for the afternoon. Instead of putting your efforts into better time management, focus on the energy level you have to complete the task.

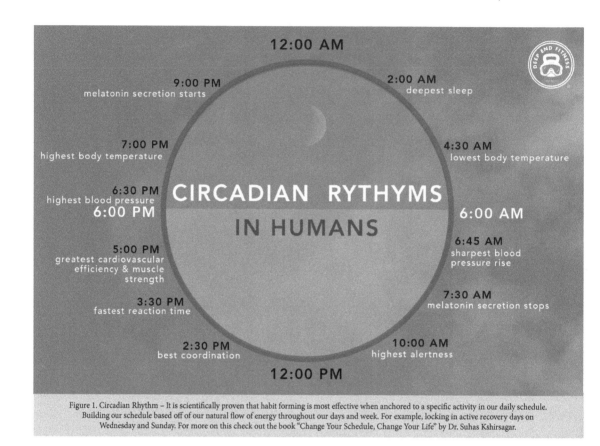

Figure 1. Circadian Rhythm – It is scientifically proven that habit forming is most effective when anchored to a specific activity in our daily schedule. Building our schedule based off of our natural flow of energy throughout our days and week. For example, locking in active recovery days on Wednesday and Sunday. For more on this check out the book "Change Your Schedule, Change Your Life" by Dr. Suhas Kshirsagar.

Eliminate distractions and clutter: Know and understand your current priority. If it's not important to you or truly serves a purpose, remove it from your life to free up your energy and efforts.

Minimizing physical and visual distractions in your workspace is one way to achieve this. If you are focused on spending time with your family or friends, put your phone in another room or switch it to "do not disturb" mode. If you are focused on a specific project at work, only check your email once or twice a day. Although answering emails is important, they can become a distraction because of the unexpected times and frequency they come in.

INTRODUCTION TO THE F.R.E.E. YOUR MIND GUIDEBOOK AND OPERATING SYSTEM

Stay within your routine: Establishing a productive and positive daily routine is beneficial to you and those around you. It provides structure, creates productive habits, and forward momentum that will carry you through your days, even if you don't have the strength to carry yourself. Once you have established a productive and positive driven routine, stick to it - this is the hardest part. Following a daily routine helps you establish and maintain priorities, limit procrastination, align with your goals, and make you mentally and physically healthier. It lowers your reliance on willpower and motivation to work towards accomplishing your goals.

Eliminate worry and concerns through discipline: As human beings we are limited by our abilities. Self-discipline comes from understanding what we are capable of and our limitations. We can't control every situation, but we should always strive to push that boundary of limitation... one step at a time.

Self-discipline is about controlling ourselves. Anything else that resides outside of us is shared by the environment around us, including people and nature.

Willpower exercises:

1. Keep a journal for 30 days. Log your intention for each day and track your goals / progress. If you miss a day, continue on but your goal should be 30 consecutive days.

2. If improving your nutrition is part of your goals, keep a food diary for 7 days or more. Take time before and after you eat to analyze how it makes you feel. Track this in your journal.

3. Spend less money. Set goals around spending and meet / exceed them. Take time to create a budget, document all expenses, and get a real sense of what your debt-to-income ratio is.

4. Create and meet your own deadlines.

5. Keep your word with yourself and others.

INTRODUCTION TO THE F.R.E.E. YOUR MIND GUIDEBOOK AND OPERATING SYSTEM

On-Demand Relaxation:

As humans, we are biologically created to be reactive instead of thinking critically and thoughtfully. Because of this, panic makes us behave emotionally and often out of fear. When the body is under stress, it enters survival mode, also known as fight-or-flight. Under these conditions, the body prepares itself by overproducing the stress hormone, cortisol. The cortisol shoots to the brain and slows down your ability to think critically. In order to combat these natural reactions, we have to be able to access our on-demand relaxation; the ability to calm our nerves, assess the situation, and develop different courses of action. Remember that you are at a great disadvantage whenever you approach a situation emotionally, rather than logically.

How do we do this? There are actions you can do before, during, and after each situation that will better prepare you to approach situations logically.

Before:
- Understand that it is natural to feel amped up during stressful situations
- Understand energy management
- Increase accountability
- Eliminate procrastination
- Practice optimism
- Meditate often
- Practice decision making exercises to work on speed and efficiency

During:
- Revert back to training
- Create a calm visualization
- Efficient breathing to calm nerves and slow heart rate (see on-demand relaxation below)

After:
- Take a second to process what happened
- Identify the gaps or flaws
- Learn from it. Let it go

As you can see, there are many ways and steps to prepare for these situations and fewer steps to manage it once it has already begun.

INTRODUCTION TO THE F.R.E.E. YOUR MIND GUIDEBOOK AND OPERATING SYSTEM

Here's an example of on-demand relaxation: Think of a big wave surfer that is going to surf one of the biggest waves of his life. He paddles out, spots the perfect swell and begins to match the speed of the wave for the long-anticipated wave. He hits the face of the wave on an off angle and goes under the massive wave. At this point he can begin to panic and fight to get to the surface for air or... he/she can understand that there are key things that can be done to survive...stay calm and relaxed as possible until the wave has passed to find the right opportunity to come up for air. As we mentioned earlier in mental focus, manage your energy in the right opportunity instead of the duration.

*DEF sponsored athlete and pro surfer Cole Houshmand

INTRODUCTION TO THE F.R.E.E. YOUR MIND GUIDEBOOK AND OPERATING SYSTEM

Economy of motion: is the concept of minimizing unnecessary movements to improve the effectiveness of effectiveness of effort. Whether this be through body movement during exercise or the pattern of life you carry during the day, minimizing unwanted effort reduces the risks of over exertion, injury, and added stress.

The first step to improving your economy of motion is to identify deficiencies and drag in your movement or pattern of life. The second step is to make an effort to remove those flaws and insufficiencies. The third step is to improve and perfect those movements until you can noticeably see and feel a difference between when you started and where you are now. The fourth and repeating step is to reassess and continuously improve your process and movement. Remember that this may not come easy and to keep an optimistic mind to see the areas you can reduce drag and improve efficiency. Key things to identify when maximizing your economy of motion:

Eliminate Drag: Properly plan for and mitigate obstacles and risks – Adapt to the situation to get back to your planned pattern of life – Find your Flow State.

For example, a swimmer pays close attention to the details in utilizing the economy of motion combined with proper body mechanics to maximize their body position, arm action, leg action, and glide to minimize drag. The ultimate goal is to move forward faster and save energy. There are multiple things that a swimmer can do to master their movement to become powerful, fast, and effective. Similarly, it's important to identify the details in your daily activities to maximize your flow.

Efficient Breathing: Every system in the body relies on oxygen. From cognition to digestion, efficient breathing gives you the ability to think clearly, reduce stress levels, boost your body's immune system, sleep better, and digest food more efficiently. We are all energy, breath is what moves energy through our body, allowing for all systems to work at a higher level.

Breathing is the most basic function and necessity of the human body. It fuels the brain and body with oxygen to help strengthen the muscles and stimulate cognitive thinking. Yet, very few people breathe properly to allow the body and mind to function the way it should. A lot of us have adapted to a way of breathing that is only enough to keep us functioning.

INTRODUCTION TO THE F.R.E.E. YOUR MIND GUIDEBOOK AND OPERATING SYSTEM

Before you can understand proper and efficient breathing techniques, let's go over the process your body takes when it takes a full breath. When you inhale, your diaphragm contracts and moves downward allowing your lungs room to expand. Your intercostal muscles, in between your ribs, contract to pull your rib cage up and outward to expand your lungs.

Air is taken in through your mouth and nose and travels through your trachea to your lungs. After passing through your bronchial tubes, the air is passed into your bloodstream through the air sacs in your lungs where it exchanges oxygen for carbon dioxide.

Let's discuss breathing efficiently. These are three things that you can fix in every breath:

- *Posture:* Sitting or standing up straight will allow the lungs to expand quickly and efficiently to exchange the oxygen and carbon dioxide in your body.

- *Full Exhale:* Most people only exhale about 70 percent of the carbon dioxide in their lungs. Try to calmly push all the air out of your lungs as though you are inflating a balloon.

- *Full Inhales:* For all breathing practices and breath holding techniques used in Deep End Fitness (DEP) or with Underwater Torpedo League (UTL) athletes, we engage our entire diaphragm from the bottom of our ribcage, up through the lungs and beyond until our shoulders rise. That is one full breath.

Now that you know how to breathe properly, these are some additional breathing exercises that you can do to improve your breathing and breath holds, control anxiety and stress, and increase athletic performance.

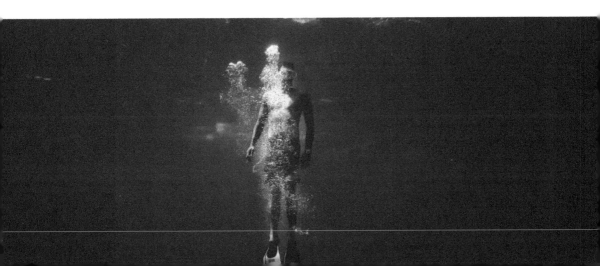

INTRODUCTION TO THE F.R.E.E. YOUR MIND GUIDEBOOK AND OPERATING SYSTEM

Basics of Low Breathing:

Low breathing promotes relaxation and creativity while chest breathing enhances fight or flight, stress, and anxiety in our brains which translates throughout our body. When we stay in fight or flight mode for too long we become ineffective and start to break down. By engaging our diaphragm and practicing deep breathing, we can control our entire nervous system.

Upper Regulation:

This is a 15-30sec breathing exercise to activate the entire diaphragm into breathing cycles; in through the nose - out through the mouth. This also activates heart rate and increases CO_2. When we exercise our CO_2 over time, we can increase our lactate threshold levels, also known as CO_2 tolerance.

Clearing Breaths:

Breathing out through your mouth until lungs and diaphragm are completely empty.

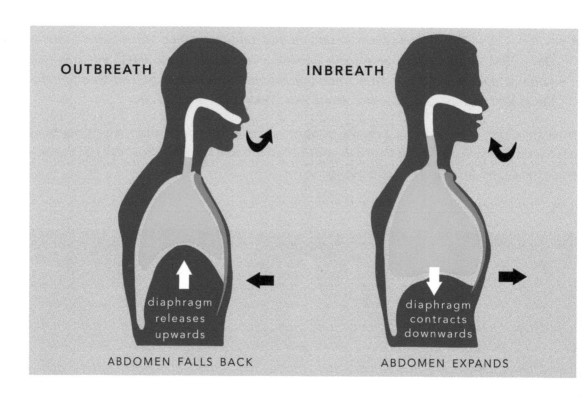

INTRODUCTION TO THE F.R.E.E. YOUR MIND GUIDEBOOK AND OPERATING SYSTEM

Triangle Breathing:
Three sec inhale through the nose, 3sec hold, 3sec exhale through the mouth. Repeat this cycle 3-5 times.

Box Breathing:
Four sec inhale through the nose, 4sec hold, 4sec exhale through the mouth, 4sec hold. Repeat the cycle 4-6 times.

Yawning Technique:
Simple tool to relax and lower your heart rate before a demanding performance.

Volumes of Air of Breath Over 60sec:
Think of how a chain smoker breathes with just their chest, 30-40 breaths in a minute with small volumes of air in each breath. Now, think of a freediver that is going down to touch 200 feet below the ocean on one breath and imagine that breath. Freedivers sometimes take up to a 25 second breath before making descent. One of the goals of this program is to take longer breaths with more volumes of air to improve your health, performance, and way of being.

WHAT YOU WILL GET
OUT OF THIS PROGRAM

The F.R.E.E. Your Mind Workbook also uses the tools of self-reflection to promote the growth mindset by first identifying gaps within your life, analyzing the key issue at hand, then reframing that issue to allow you the user to see it from a different perspective. Once you have seen the problem through a different lens, strategically plan different options to re-attack the problem set. In this process we will identify and use the key attributes to help strengthen the relationship you have with yourself and others to provide clarity and de-clutter mental baggage. The end goal is to come to self actualization by taking a deep dive into yourself to understand your motivations, limits, and how to overcome boundaries. We do this by creating less drag and improving efficiency in your everyday life from breathing, business, relationships and creating a positive outlook on the world.

KEY COMPONENTS TO CONSIDER DURING REFLECTION

Reflective thinking requires you to identify, understand and to define the knowledge and experience you bring to each new situation, to make the connections based on the insight you have from past learning and experience, and bring these to new situations. Through this process you become a critical thinker and active learner. Throughout this workbook you will strategically assess yourself and your ability to identify gaps, game plan, practice positive self-talk, and celebrate wins. We will use these key attributes to determine the areas that need to be maintained or improved on in showing up for yourself. These attributes consist of: Effort, Accountability, Performance, Self-Confidence, Consistency, Discipline, "Calm in the Clutch", Setting Boundaries, Ability to Surrender, and Flow. You will also reflect and assess your ability to show up for your people; your family, friends, and co-workers.

Effort

Effort is the vigorous or determined attempt to achieve something. There must be an amount of effort put into a task to see results. It is likely that the more you put in, the better the outcome can become. Although the amount of effort we put into a project or relationship does not always guarantee success, it significantly increases the probability.

An example of effort is using your brain to develop and carry out a plan. Give yourself enough time to assess the risks, come up with different courses of action, select the best one, and run with it. These actions take effort and the more you put into each action, the more chances of success you will have.

WHAT YOU WILL GET
OUT OF THIS PROGRAM

Accountability

Accountability is described as accepting responsibility for one's words and actions. It can be with yourself and others. Accountability eliminates the time and effort you spend on unnecessary activities and other unproductive behavior. Accountability starts with you. As you hold others accountable, you must also hold yourself accountable. When you make people accountable for their actions, you're effectively training them to understand the value of their work. When done right, accountability can increase your and your team members' skills and confidence.

TOOLS FOR ACCOUNTABILITY:

Self-Accountability: Self-accountability is the act of showing up for yourself each and every day. Self- accountability is the cornerstone of morals and ethics. It is who you are and what you do when no one is watching. When you have a well-developed sense of self-accountability, you are honest with yourself and are answerable and responsible for your words and actions. This workbook will challenge you to hold yourself accountable everyday not just with your words or actions to others but most importantly to yourself. Hold yourself accountable and you will take control of your life.

Accountability Coach: An accountability coach is a person who you hold yourself accountable to each week for getting things done, meeting your deadlines, and achieving your goals. Saying what you want out loud or writing it down demonstrates intent to do the task. Having someone to help keep you on track increases the likelihood of those things actually happening. Not only throughout this workbook but in life, find a mentor, someone you look up to, or a close friend that you can discuss your goals with and ask them to hold you accountable for your words and intended actions.

Training Partners: Some people are able to work, set goals, and exercise alone and stay focused. For others, a training partner (in life, workouts, business, or a good friend) will boost their motivation and overall performance for that specific action. A sense of healthy competition can prevail between you and your partner, which will keep not only your fitness and work ethic levels high, but give you a support system to fall back on.

WHAT YOU WILL GET
OUT OF THIS PROGRAM

Performance

A performance mindset is achievable by everyone regardless of experience, gender, age, ethnicity, or social class. It is not only for the intellectually or athletically gifted person, but rather the ability to create the highest internal processes to perform as the best version of yourself. Your performance mindset is one that is authentic to you, simultaneously structured for your individual situations and what you are encountering. You have to remember that your performance is based on your life experiences and the level of knowledge you have regarding a specific area of your life. Rather than comparing your performance with others, compare it to your own past performance and how you can do better this time around. We are in competition with ourselves first.

Self Confidence

To be confident means feeling sure of your abilities and yourself. This doesn't mean being presumptuous, but instead confident in capabilities. It is a self-reflection about your knowledge and abilities and awareness that you are capable of anything if you put your mind to it. Confidence empowers you to feel prepared for everyday challenges. The best way to be confident is to be prepared, understand your abilities and how to apply them in the right time and place. If you are not confident in yourself, who can truly be confident in you?

Consistency

A consistent person is someone who always acts in the same way, has the same outlook on life, treats people with the same respect or attitude, puts in the same amount of effort into something, and typically accomplishes the same level of success in what they put their minds and hearts into. Consistency develops habits which in turn build momentum.

A habit becomes second nature through consistent, dedicated application to self and self- reflection. Make it important and plan for it. Habits make or break you... ritualize, ritualize, ritualize.

Discipline

Discipline is the practice of making yourself and/or other people follow a set of standards or behaviour. It is the aspect of following, behaving, and working in a controlled way. Nothing worthwhile in life comes easy. If you want it bad enough, you must be prepared to work for it, to fight for it, to give up everything for it. If it's worth the prize, it's worth the fight. Self discipline is how you control and manage the outcome of the goals you have set for yourself.

WHAT YOU WILL GET OUT OF THIS PROGRAM

"Calm in the Clutch"

The truth is that some people cave under pressure. Regardless of myths that we will rise to the occasion, most people don't perform as well as they think under pressure. No matter the task, pressure diminishes our decision-making process, attention span, physical and emotional dexterity, and perception; whether it be in the sports arena, during a business presentation, or in your personal life. In order to minimize the effects of pressure on our performance, we must be prepared mentally through practice and rehearsals, focusing on the task not the outcome, realizing this is just one of many opportunities; positive self-talk, and working on our flaws and weak points early on.

Throughout this workbook you will explore different ways to identify unnecessary drag and things to improve for yourself and those around you. Once you have identified where and how to improve, you can begin to build strategies you can use to reduce pressure and allow you to excel in whatever you do and perform when it matters the most.

Setting Boundaries

Set boundaries on anything that creates drag or holds you back from reaching your true potential and happiness. People around us can be toxic and create drag for us by which holds us back from reaching our true potential. Some activities or habits can be toxic as well and create drag. By being self-aware and accountable of our behaviors and actions, we can make decisions that create flow in our lives. At the same time, we set boundaries where needed to prevent drag and increase flow.

Ability to Surrender

As there are many things within ourselves that we can control, there are so many more that we cannot. We must be able to identify the ones we can't control, surrender to them, and let go. Control is a result of being attached to a specific outcome that we think at the moment is the best for us, but that is not always the case. The real case is that the energy of surrender accomplishes much more than the energy of control. Surrendering in spirituality is allowing yourself to be with what is right in front of you. If it's talking to a friend, then surrender to it and talk to your friend. If it's needed quality time with your family when you have work to do, spend time with your family, work can wait. Surrender means to feel, to live in the moment.

WHAT YOU WILL GET OUT OF THIS PROGRAM

Flow

Achieving flow is ultimately about leading a more enjoyable, happier life. When we are in flow, we are challenging ourselves, somewhere in between boredom and panic. We cannot perform at our highest level if we don't challenge ourselves. We cannot stay at that level or continue to evolve without remembering to relax. Recovery is also key to anyone that performs at a high level in their job or in fitness, sports, etc.

Showing Up for Others

Showing up for others is the core of creating and maintaining strong and meaningful bonds with friends, family, and coworkers. It is what turns the people you know into your people. Showing up for the people we care about means being there in their moments of happiness, pain, suffering, and when they are truly themselves. We do this by communicating to them that they are not alone and that someone understands them in this world.

Showing up might sound simple, but it's definitely not easy. It requires a lot of hard work, dedication, and it's not always pretty. Being there for someone you care about requires a lot of confidence, emotional intelligence, generosity, willingness to be vulnerable, and most importantly effort. And really showing up for others requires you to show up for yourself first. That means really understanding yourself, taking care of your mental and physical health, and setting boundaries.

Showing up for yourself will give you the ability to be more present for others and allow you to be a better friend, family member, and coworker. It will give you the capacity to be aware, control, understand and express your emotions around others. It gives you the ability to handle interpersonal relationships empathetically. Once you are able to do that, it will prevent one-sided relationships that can prevent resentment and build up negative aggression.

As we strive to be people to show up for others, we have to recognize how others have shown up for us and use it as examples of its life-saving power. And the more of us who regularly show up for each other, the more contagious our light becomes, and the brighter the world becomes.

TRAINING TRUTHS

No Egos

As coaches we always train from an egoless coaching perspective, we also encourage our students and athletes to leave their egos behind to break barriers and limits. This allows us to share vulnerability with each other and unlock true power and potential. When we lead with our egos, the walls are up and mentally we are not able to go all in 100%, or even be fully accountable with how we really think, feel, and experience life.

Quality Over Quantity

Focusing on quality rather than quantity tends to bring more rewarding results in our lives. By choosing to give more effort for quality results versus the number of results within any area of your life, you automatically open yourself up to experience the true efficiency with which you can experience meaning. Choosing quality over quantity leads you to the straightest path towards contentment and meaning.

For example, within the U.S. Special Operations community, there is a truth; quality over quantity. It refers to a small number of carefully selected, well trained, and well led people who are preferred over larger numbers of troops; some of whom may not be up to the task. Special Operators are considered 'force multipliers'. They work in small teams (12 or less) and have the capabilities of a much larger force. This capability stems from the quality of those who serve on a Special Forces team. They are lean, highly trained and highly effective.

Flow is the Balance of Challenge and Skill

This is us "in the zone". This doesn't happen unless we are placing ourselves into challenges that align with our skills and will bring out the best in us even if they are going to take work. Identify what challenges will lead you to your goals and create a process: crawl, walk, run, fly and execute your process and make any changes as needed. Trust the process.

Sacrifice

Real success is never without sacrifice. It is the act of giving up something that you want in order to achieve something else. Discomfort is going to be part of reaching your true potential. In building a dream and accomplishing your goals, you are going to be stretched in your path to your own greatness. Your biggest breakdowns can lead to your biggest breakthroughs. Understanding what you are giving up and why is key.

TRAINING TRUTHS

Pay Attention to What Your Mind and Body is Telling You

Our bodies and minds constantly send us messages about its internal conditions. We need to be able to recognize, understand, and listen to these signs. Subtle cues are often offered about what we need in forms of a gut feeling when we know something is right or wrong, shivers when we are cold, or a yawn when we are tired. Other times it sends signals through an allergic skin reaction, loss of sleep, or being extremely irritable. With so many other things we have going on, it's easy to lose sight of these signals from our body and minds telling us what we really need.

Listening to your mind and body simply means you regularly pause to feel. Pause for one second to take a breath, relax, and be open to what signals you feel and ask yourself what do you need right now. Analyze the situation and develop different ways to improve the situation. It might just be to get a full night of sleep if you're over exerting yourself at work or school. Once you have a plan, don't be afraid to ask for help. Always remember to maximize your flow to reduce unnecessary stress and overloading your body and mind.

SELF-REFLECTION

Self-reflection helps to build emotional self-awareness. By taking the time to ask ourselves the important questions, we gain a better understanding of our emotions, goals, strengths, weaknesses and what drives us. When we want to improve our flow and achieve our goals, we need to see three things clearly:

1. What are you trying to do?

2. What are you actually doing?

3. What can you do to bridge the gap between them?

Reflection is a powerful improvement tool; it gives us the ability to think back, observe ourselves in action, and learn from it. Everyday we experience new things that are different than those we have previously encountered in our lives. We are never just spectators to those experiences because during, we thought, felt, acted (or did not act), during these experiences. Sometimes, we are not mindful of what happened, so we miss the learning experience and benefits from that situation. If we don't pay attention, we miss the opportunity to learn and grow. Use these steps to help break down the self-reflection process:

1. REFLECT ON YOUR EXPERIENCE.

- Think about what happened and what your actions, thoughts, and feelings were at that time.

- Was there anything significant about what happened that stood out more than others?

- Were there any emotions triggered? If so, what caused this?

2. REFLECT ON WHAT YOU LEARNED.

- Analyze your experience and compare it to past experiences or lessons.

- What can I learn and take away from this experience?

3. APPLY TO THE FUTURE.

- How can you apply this moving forward?

- What additional options do you have the next time you encounter a similar situation?

- What specifically do I intend to do based on my reflection?

SELF-REFLECTION

During the course of this workbook you will be asked to self-reflect on your past and present experiences, thought process, actions, goals, and intentions in key areas of your life.

You will use the key attributes of: Effort, Accountability, Performance, Self Confidence, Consistency, Discipline, "Calm in the Clutch", Setting Boundaries, Ability to Surrender, and Flow to self reflect on how you show up for yourself throughout the week. Give yourself a score of 1- 10 in each area.

Throughout this workbook we will also reflect on how we can show up for others focusing on three different groups of people: your family, friends, and work team. Give yourself a score of 1-10 in each group.

Be honest with yourself, there are no right or wrong answers and the scale is based on you and your ability to look within yourself to seek self improvement for your people. If you don't know the right score, don't be afraid to ask your people within those groups.

WEEK 1 ASSESSMENT/ CRAWL PHASE

GOALS AND GAPS / SELF-ASSESMENT

Most of us involved with this program are performance-based and focused by nature. We assess flow to be in the middle or somewhere in between boredom and panic. How much are you holding back from challenging yourself to create more flow? Setting intentions, realizations, and affirmations sets up for success in aligning with our true potential and experience. How can you declutter your mind, your life, and your schedule to strategically align with your purpose and your goal. Most importantly, how are you holding yourself accountable with your goals? Choose someone in your life that you respect and nominate them as your accountability coach for this month. If not, look into coaching with one of our Elite Coaches at www.deependfitness.com

Goals and Gaps Exercise: Fill out the exercise below in the simplest, most focused answers possible. To maximize effectiveness, ensure each goal is : Specific, Measurable, Attainable, Relevant, and Timely. Widely known as S.M.A.R.T. goals.

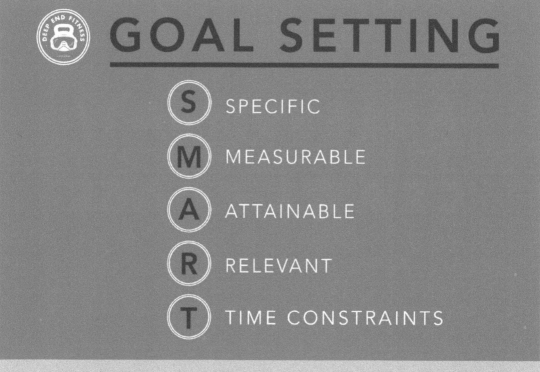

GOAL SETTING

- **S** SPECIFIC
- **M** MEASURABLE
- **A** ATTAINABLE
- **R** RELEVANT
- **T** TIME CONSTRAINTS

Figure 2. SMART Goals – Making our goals quantifiable and achievable greatly enhance likelihood of success. SMART goals also anchor us into a decision-making process.

WEEK 1 CRAWL PHASE

PROFESSIONAL

Biggest accomplishment to date:

_____
_____
_____
_____
_____

Biggest goal moving forward:

_____
_____
_____
_____
_____
_____

What's the Gap?

_____
_____
_____
_____
_____

FAMILY

Biggest accomplishment to date:

_____
_____
_____
_____

Biggest goal moving forward:

_____
_____
_____
_____
_____

WEEK 1 CRAWL PHASE

What's the Gap?

_____
_____
_____
_____
_____

PERSONAL EDUCATION
Biggest accomplishment to date:

_____
_____
_____
_____
_____

Biggest goal moving forward:

_____
_____
_____
_____
_____

What's the Gap?

_____
_____
_____
_____
_____

HOBBY AND LEISURE
Biggest accomplishment to date:

_____
_____
_____
_____
_____

WEEK 1 CRAWL PHASE

Biggest goal moving forward:

_____

_____

_____

_____

_____

What's the Gap?

_____

_____

_____

_____

PURPOSE / GLOBAL IMPACT
Biggest accomplishment to date:

_____

_____

_____

_____

Biggest goal moving forward:

_____

_____

_____

_____

What's the Gap?

_____

_____

_____

_____

WEEK 1 CRAWL PHASE

OVERALL REFLECTION

Do you have any similarities in your gaps or goals?

_____
_____
_____
_____
_____

What were the biggest common trends that you have recognized throughout this exercise?

_____
_____
_____
_____
_____

How can you develop an action plan to achieve or combine your goals to maximize efficiency?

_____
_____
_____
_____
_____

MENTAL FOCUS / EXPANSION

What are your top three personal goals this quarter, this year?

_____
_____
_____
_____
_____
_____
_____

WEEK 1 CRAWL PHASE

Time assessment:

Break down your day on Monday with how much you spend doing each activity that you do. Be honest with yourself as far as how much time you spend on your phone, working out, cooking, being creative, anything that you do.

_____

_____

_____

_____

_____

People, Places, Things Assessment:

What people, places and things or activities in your day / week are serving you?

_____

_____

_____

_____

_____

What people, places, and things or activities are not serving you?

_____

_____

_____

_____

_____

What are the things you want to release from bothering you to create less drag and add more flow?

_____

_____

_____

_____

_____

_____

WEEK 1 CRAWL PHASE

ON DEMAND RELAXATION / ENERGY

How much time do you spend in "go" mode during your day?

_____

_____

_____

_____

_____

How much time do you spend in "relax" mode during your day?

_____

_____

_____

_____

_____

What is your on and off switch in between modes?

_____

_____

_____

_____

_____

How do you recharge your battery? (alone or with others)

_____

_____

_____

_____

_____

What is your most fulfilling creative outlet these days?

_____

_____

_____

_____

_____

WEEK 1 CRAWL PHASE

How much reading do you do?

_____
_____
_____
_____
_____

Any other leisure / hobbies that restore you?

_____
_____
_____
_____
_____

What does your fitness regimen look like?

_____
_____
_____
_____
_____

What does your nutrition look like?

_____
_____
_____
_____

How are you evolving yourself spiritually?

_____
_____
_____
_____
_____

WEEK 1 CRAWL PHASE

How much sleep are you getting?

_____

_____

_____

_____

_____

How often do you meditate?

_____

_____

_____

_____

_____

Do you keep a journal?

_____

_____

_____

_____

_____

Are there any parts of your routine now that you feel you need to change or modify to increase effectiveness? *(Law of Accommodation)*

_____

_____

_____

_____

_____

ECONOMY OF MOTION
What does your daily routine look like at home? At work?

_____

_____

_____

_____

_____

WEEK 1 CRAWL PHASE

Are there any unnecessary activities that adds additional stress or time to your schedule?

_____

_____

_____

_____

_____

_____

WEEK 1 CRAWL PHASE

What does your daily routine look like on the road?

_____
_____
_____
_____
_____

What is your pattern of life throughout your day / week and how can you make it flow better? For example, how can you move or stack activities that would allow your week / days to flow better? How could you streamline your meetings or do less to get more out of your work days. _(Law of Least Effort)_

_____
_____
_____
_____
_____

EFFICIENT BREATHING
How often are you breathing in with your diaphragm vs. chest breathing?

_____
_____
_____
_____

On average, how many breaths do you take over a minute, and are they long and deep breaths or shallow?

_____
_____
_____
_____

WEEK 1 CRAWL PHASE

After breathing all of your air out, how many seconds (maxing out) can you breathe in from the bottom of your stomach until your shoulders rise and you are completely full of air?

_____

_____

_____

_____

_____

What is your max breath hold on land? (Use breathing exercises to warm up. pg 9)

_____

_____

_____

_____

WEEK 1 WRAP-UP

"Rome was not built in a day, but they were laying bricks every hour."
- James Clear

Stay humble and continue to press. Sometimes under stress, we can have breakdowns. This is when we get upset or lose control of our emotions. Every breakdown that we have is intelligence that we can use to break through. Focus on the realizations you are having and recognize your strengths/weaknesses and where they come from. Appreciate that you have accomplished Week 1 of this process moving into Week 2. Trust the process.

Phase 1 was a Self Assessment Week.
Answer the following questions honestly below:

Rate your current performance overall in your life:

_____
_____
_____
_____
_____

Personal - How have you shown up for yourself?

_____
_____
_____
_____
_____

Professional - How have you shown up to others?

_____
_____
_____
_____

Family- How have you shown up for your family?

_____
_____
_____
_____
_____

WEEK 1 WRAP-UP

Where do you see yourself being in the next 30-90 days?

_____

_____

_____

_____

Who is your accountability coach? If you have not done so already, assign a person in your life that you respect that you can share your goals with that will hold you accountable. This can also be a workout buddy, but they must hold you accountable so choose this person wisely, or you can select one of our DEF Coaches.

_____

_____

_____

_____

_____

WEEK 1 SELF-REFLECTION SCORES

On a scale of 1 - 10, rate how you showed up for yourself this week in each of these key attributes.

Effort:
1 2 3 4 5 6 7 8 9 10

Accountability:
1 2 3 4 5 6 7 8 9 10

Performance:
1 2 3 4 5 6 7 8 9 10

Self-Confidence:
1 2 3 4 5 6 7 8 9 10

Consistency:
1 2 3 4 5 6 7 8 9 10

Discipline:
1 2 3 4 5 6 7 8 9 10

"Calm in the Clutch":
1 2 3 4 5 6 7 8 9 10

Setting Boundaries:
1 2 3 4 5 6 7 8 9 10

Ability to Surrender:
1 2 3 4 5 6 7 8 9 10

Flow:
1 2 3 4 5 6 7 8 9 10

On a scale of 1 - 10, rate how you showed up for your people this week in each of these key attributes.

Family:
1 2 3 4 5 6 7 8 9 10

Friends:
1 2 3 4 5 6 7 8 9 10

Coworkers:
1 2 3 4 5 6 7 8 9 10

WEEK 2
WALK PHASE

DEEP END FITNESS

WEEK 2 WALK PHASE

What we call "glass ceilings" are the preconceived notions that we carry, also known as "programming," that limit us from achieving our ultimate potential. Once we unlock a glass ceiling (say, holding your breath for 2 minutes) when you thought you could NEVER do that. What else "can't" you do now when you know you actually can. Continue to make your life a challenge, a sports team tryout, or being assessed for progress everyday.

Remember back to the Week 1 Wrap Up and the answers that you have written down on how you show up for yourself and your people.

How much real effort are you putting into your development / experience?

_____
_____
_____
_____
_____

How are you setting yourself up with Confidence Targets? (A confidence target is a milestone set up on the path towards your goal that builds confidence and reinforces commitment in yourself and in the process.)

_____
_____
_____
_____
_____

What are your systematic processes for how you are reaching your goals and setting yourself up for success? (Remember, Flow is the balance of challenge and skill.)

_____
_____
_____
_____
_____

WEEK 2 WALK PHASE

What are the top three things you learned about yourself in Week 1 related to your goals and where you want to be at the end of the month? End of the quarter? End of the year?

_____

_____

_____

_____

_____

What can you do this week to declutter your mind?

_____

_____

_____

_____

What can you do this week to declutter your living/work area?

_____

_____

_____

_____

_____

What can you do this week to declutter (maybe replace with "streamline) your routine/habits?

_____

_____

_____

_____

_____

WEEK 2 WALK PHASE

What small changes are you making to create more flow and less drag with you activities to help you focus on the things that are most important to you?

_____

_____

_____

_____

_____

Is there anything else you can adjust to improve the pathway to meeting and exceeding your goals?

_____

_____

_____

_____

_____

ON- DEMAND RELAXATION / ENERGY

What are the top three things you learned about yourself in Week 1 regarding you life balance between being "on" go-mode at work, fitness, at home, etc. and your "of switch" being in relaxation mode?

_____

_____

_____

_____

_____

List below the action steps you will implement this week to create balance:
A. Three changes in your daily routine to add more balance related to on and off switch:

_____

_____

_____

_____

_____

WEEK 2 WALK PHASE

B. Three changes in your week to create more flow and less drag with your activities

_____
_____
_____
_____
_____

How are you going to change your nutrition to align more with your goals?

_____
_____
_____
_____

How are you going to change your schedule this week to make sure you are recharging your battery?

_____
_____
_____
_____
_____

How is your workout routine changing this week?

_____
_____
_____
_____

How are you going to increase your rest time, sleep, and meditation to de-clutter your mind and recover at a higher level?

_____
_____
_____
_____

WEEK 2 WALK PHASE

How are you going to charge yourself spiritually this week? (This can even be going out into nature and spending time looking at certain things that interest you.)

_____

_____

_____

_____

_____

What reading are you going to pick up that is related to a hobby that you are interested in, your goals, or something new that you have always wanted to learn about?

_____

_____

_____

_____

_____

How are you mixing up your training to ensure that you are not getting stuck in the "law of accommodation"? Once it becomes routine or comfortable it stops being as effective.

_____

_____

_____

_____

_____

What people, places, and activities are you changing this week to add more flow / less drag in your life?

_____

_____

_____

_____

_____

WEEK 2 WALK PHASE

n your own words, what were the biggest realizations you had from the work you did
n Week 1?

_____

_____

_____

_____

_____

s there anything else not covered above that you would like to implement this week
from the realizations you had last week?

_____

_____

_____

_____

How are you keeping yourself accountable with your goals? Being honest with yourself
and writing them down. Tell your accountability coach and we also recommend that
you tell close people in your circle that you trust and respect.

_____

_____

_____

_____

Lastly, a useful tool for success in this program is keeping a journal. How can you / are
you using a journal to stay accountable, creative, and consistent with yourself? This
can be a notebook or dedicated notes app on your phone; whatever works for you.
Make a new habit to write daily to increase your effectiveness with the program.

_____

_____

_____

_____

_____

WEEK 2 WALK PHASE

ECONOMY OF MOTION

What were the biggest realizations in Week 1 about your schedule that create drag for you in your daily flow? In your week?

_____
_____
_____
_____
_____

List the changes you are going to make daily and weekly to increase the flow in your schedule

_____
_____
_____
_____
_____

How is your pattern of life / economy of motion throughout your day /week going to change to make it flow better? Remember, less is more.

_____
_____
_____
_____
_____

EFFICIENT BREATHING

What was the maximum breath, in seconds, you took in Week 1?

_____
_____
_____
_____
_____
_____
_____
_____

WEEK 2 WALK PHASE

What was your maximum breath hold, in seconds, on land in Week 1?

_____

_____

_____

_____

_____

What is your goal for each week? By Week 4?

_____

_____

_____

_____

_____

Record how many breaths in do you take over a minute this week during normal breathing.

_____

_____

_____

_____

_____

WEEK 2 WRAP-UP

> **"If you can't measure it, you can't improve it."**
> **-Peter Drucker**

Once we are able to be open and honest with ourselves and others, we can get an accurate baseline about our performance. As we get to declutter our lives and our minds of activities, people and habits that are not aligned with our true purpose or goals, we can focus on the things that strategically matter to us. When we get rid of drag we create more economy of motion in our lives, with our schedules, and realize how much we can get done in shorter times. When we are in a full economy of motion we enter the Flow state. Trust the process. It will serve you well.

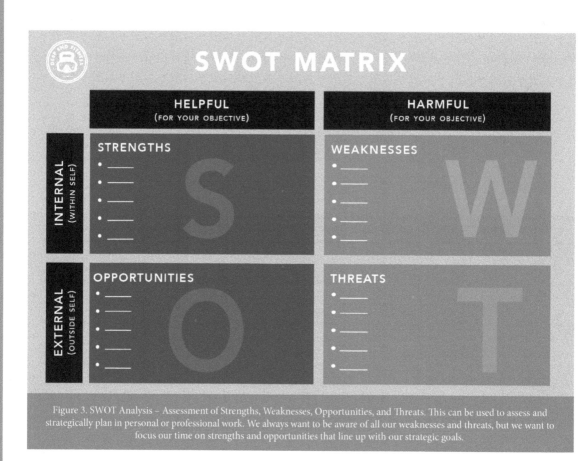

Figure 3. SWOT Analysis – Assessment of Strengths, Weaknesses, Opportunities, and Threats. This can be used to assess and strategically plan in personal or professional work. We always want to be aware of all our weaknesses and threats, but we want to focus our time on strengths and opportunities that line up with our strategic goals.

WEEK 2 WRAP-UP

FEAR RELEASE EXERCISE

What are the top three fears that hold you back from reaching your goals or ultimate performance? (Example: Fear of failure.)

Fear 1

_____

_____

_____

_____

Fear 2

_____

_____

_____

_____

Fear 3

_____

_____

_____

_____

Talk to your accountability buddy or coach about your fears and what you are committed to doing to face your fears in order to reach your goals moving forward. Remember to celebrate your small victories and continue to assess what is working for you and what is not. Most importantly, continue to find your balance between work and rest.

WEEK 2 SELF-REFLECTION SCORES

On a scale of 1 - 10, rate how you showed up for yourself this week in each of these key attributes.

Effort:
1 2 3 4 5 6 7 8 9 10

Accountability:
1 2 3 4 5 6 7 8 9 10

Performance:
1 2 3 4 5 6 7 8 9 10

Self-Confidence:
1 2 3 4 5 6 7 8 9 10

Consistency:
1 2 3 4 5 6 7 8 9 10

Discipline:
1 2 3 4 5 6 7 8 9 10

"Calm in the Clutch":
1 2 3 4 5 6 7 8 9 10

Setting Boundaries:
1 2 3 4 5 6 7 8 9 10

Ability to Surrender:
1 2 3 4 5 6 7 8 9 10

Flow:
1 2 3 4 5 6 7 8 9 10

On a scale of 1 - 10, rate how you showed up for your people this week in each of these key attributes.

Family:
1 2 3 4 5 6 7 8 9 10

Friends:
1 2 3 4 5 6 7 8 9 10

Coworkers:
1 2 3 4 5 6 7 8 9 10

WEEK 3
RUN PHASE

WEEK 3 RUN PHASE

In swimming, any movement that slows us down, be it an extra movement or bad movement, will create drag. This drag can slow us down or stop us from moving through the water. Drag stops us from reaching flow states. This week, focus on what boundaries you need to set on anything that creates drag. We also think of drag as anything that holds you back from becoming the best version of yourself, with the best performance and experience. Pay attention to what your body and mind is telling you. If you haven't already, take time to slow down – get out of reaction mode. This is also built to help you shift from fear and scarcity mindset into abundance and possibility mindset of breaking through your own glass ceilings and performing at the highest levels of your potential.

MENTAL FOCUS / EXPANSION
What are the top three things you learned or realized about yourself in the last two weeks, or since you started Week 1 of the program?

_____

_____

_____

_____

_____

Off the top of your head, what are the biggest changes that you have made that have made the most impact?

_____

_____

_____

_____

_____

Have your goals changed since starting Week 1? If so, how?

_____

_____

_____

_____

_____

WEEK 3 RUN PHASE

Restate and Redefine your top three strategic goals for the 90 days below:
What changes have you made to declutter your mind, your area of focus, and your routine to focus more on priorities that align with your goals? What can you do to further your improvements?

_____

_____

_____

_____

_____

What changes have made the biggest difference in creating more flow / less drag with your activities to help you focus on the things that are most important to you? What can you do to further those changes to increase performance and mental health?

_____

_____

_____

_____

What is anything else not listed above you have identified within the last two weeks that has helped you or you have noticed is working for you now that you were not doing before you started Week 1 of the program?

_____

_____

_____

_____

_____

_____

_____

_____

WEEK 3 RUN PHASE

ON- DEMAND RELAXATION / ENERGY

What are the three biggest changes you have made to create life balance between being "on" in your go-mode at work, fitness, at home, etc. and your "off switch" being in relaxation mode?

_____

_____

_____

_____

_____

What routines, rituals, or habits are you practicing ensuring you maintain your balance?

_____

_____

_____

_____

What areas do you see resistance in locking in these habits and going back to old patterns? Be honest with yourself.

_____

_____

_____

_____

_____

_____

_____

_____

_____

_____

_____

_____

_____

WEEK 3 RUN PHASE

For repetition, list out below the changes to implement those changes this week to create balance. If they are similar to last week make sure you re-define what they are and why they are important to you this week.

A. Three changes in your daily routine to add more balance related to regulating your on and off switch?

_____

_____

_____

_____

_____

_____

B. Three changes in your week to create more flow / less drag with your activities:

_____

_____

_____

_____

_____

_____

How have you / are you changing your nutrition to align more with your goals?

_____

_____

_____

_____

_____

How has your workout routine changed since starting Week 1 and what is your focus or priorities of work this week? This month?

_____

_____

_____

_____

_____

_____

WEEK 3 RUN PHASE

How have you increased your rest time, sleep, and meditation to declutter your mind and recover at a higher level? What is working best for you? What are you having the most resistance with?

_____

_____

_____

_____

_____

How charged are you spiritually? What have you done that has elevated your spirit these last two weeks and what is your focus this week? (This can even be going out into nature and spending time looking at certain things that interest you.)

_____

_____

_____

_____

_____

What reading are you doing this week?

_____

_____

_____

_____

What are the creative outlets that are working for you? What, if any, would you like to add before Week 4 "Fly Phase"?

_____

_____

_____

_____

_____

_____

_____

WEEK 3 RUN PHASE

How have you mixed up your training schedule to ensure that you are not getting stuck in the "law of accommodation" principle that once it becomes routine or comfortable it stops being as effective.

_____
_____
_____
_____

What people, places, and activities have you changed this month to add more flow/less drag in your life?

_____
_____
_____
_____

How are you keeping yourself accountable with your goals? What people in your circle have you shared your progress, commitments, and goals with?

_____
_____
_____
_____

Lastly – A big trend with success in this program is keeping a journal. How can you / are you using a journal to stay accountable, creative, and consistent with yourself? This can be a notebook or dedicated notes app on your phone whatever works for you. Write in it daily to increase your effectiveness with the program.

_____
_____
_____
_____

Anything else you would like to add that is not listed above?

_____
_____
_____
_____

WEEK 3 RUN PHASE

ECONOMY OF MOTION

What were the biggest realizations from the last two weeks about your schedule that create drag for you in your daily flow and in your week? List your top three below.

_____

_____

_____

_____

_____

What changes have you made to increase the flow in your schedule on a daily and weekly scale?

_____

_____

_____

_____

_____

How can you strategically plan or make adjustments to your pattern of life (movement) throughout your day / week to make it flow even better? Remember, less is more.

_____

_____

_____

_____

_____

_____

EFFICIENT BREATHING

What was your maximum amount of breaths you took in one minute in Week 2?

_____

_____

_____

_____

_____

_____

_____

WEEK 3 RUN PHASE

What was your maximum breath hold on land (in seconds)?

_____

_____

_____

_____

_____

What is your breath hold goal this week? And moving into Week 4?

_____

_____

_____

_____

_____

_____

WEEK 3 RUN PHASE

Record how many breaths in do you take over a minute this week during normal breathing. Remember to breathe in using your entire diaphragm from the bottom of your stomach all the way up into your chest until your shoulders rise. This will enhance relaxation and creativity. Shallow breathing with only your chest increases stress, anxiety, and "fight or flight" emotional state.

WEEK 3 WRAP-UP

"A disciplined mind leads to happiness, and an undisciplined mind leads to suffering."
-Dalai Lama XIV

Remaining disciplined and being accountable to yourself and to others creates a positive shift in any relationship. It takes the average person 66 days to lock in a new habit or change a behavior. When we let go of the habits and people that don't serve us and instead have the discipline to remain accountable to our daily routines, habits, and affirmations we enhance our probability of success in reaching our goals. If we choose to be undisciplined, it will lead to the kind of suffering the Dalai Lama says.

Figure 4. Discipline/Flow/Surrender – Maintaining mental and physical discipline is foundational in our evolution. Once we lock in discipline and give ourselves the proper amount of challenge that aligns with our skills the last step is surrendering. Surrender anything that creates drag, even self-limiting beliefs or "glass ceilings" that you have from before.

WEEK 3 RUN PHASE

We are now three quarters of the way through the 30 day program.

Focus- Have you been able to declutter different areas in your life or mind?

_____
_____
_____
_____
_____

Relaxation - What key activities that recharge your battery? Name top 3.

_____
_____
_____
_____
_____

Economy of motion - How have you changed your schedule or routine to add flow?

_____
_____
_____
_____
_____

Efficient Breathing - How has your breathing changed since you started week 1 program? How are you breathing when you find yourself under stress?

_____
_____
_____
_____
_____
_____
_____
_____

WEEK 3 SELF-REFLECTION SCORES

On a scale of 1 - 10, rate how you showed up for yourself this week in each of these key attributes.

Effort:
1 2 3 4 5 6 7 8 9 10

Accountability:
1 2 3 4 5 6 7 8 9 10

Performance:
1 2 3 4 5 6 7 8 9 10

Self-Confidence:
1 2 3 4 5 6 7 8 9 10

Consistency:
1 2 3 4 5 6 7 8 9 10

Discipline:
1 2 3 4 5 6 7 8 9 10

"Calm in the Clutch":
1 2 3 4 5 6 7 8 9 10

Setting Boundaries:
1 2 3 4 5 6 7 8 9 10

Ability to Surrender:
1 2 3 4 5 6 7 8 9 10

Flow:
1 2 3 4 5 6 7 8 9 10

On a scale of 1 - 10, rate how you showed up for your people this week in each of these key attributes.

Family:
1 2 3 4 5 6 7 8 9 10

Friends:
1 2 3 4 5 6 7 8 9 10

Coworkers:
1 2 3 4 5 6 7 8 9 10

WEEK 4
FLY PHASE

WEEK 4 FLY PHASE

We hope that by now you have started to form new habits, rituals, self-talk, and affirmations that are becoming a routine. Remember that sacrifices and consistency are keys to continuing to evolve as you apply the principles of Focus, Relaxation, and Economy of Motion, and Efficient Breathing in ways that apply to YOU that work / flow with your individual performance. Remember that we are only in competition with ourselves. Take time to celebrate YOUR wins and build out your program for the next 30 days. Go Deep. Live Empowered!

MENTAL FOCUS / EXPANSION

What do you need to do in order to see your big-ticket resolutions come to fruition?

_____
_____
_____
_____
_____
_____

What steps do you need to take?

_____
_____
_____
_____
_____

What have you done that has worked in the past few weeks and what has not?

_____
_____
_____
_____
_____

Plan your weeks out on the weekend and check in with yourself bi-weekly to check and assess progress in all areas of F.R.E.E. Remember to Ritualize, Ritualize, Ritualize.

_____
_____
_____
_____
_____

WEEK 4 FLY PHASE

What are the top three things you have learned about yourself or realizations in the last month, or since you started Week 1 of the F.R.E.E. Program?

_____
_____
_____
_____
_____

Who is the best accountability partner / coach or coaches moving forward to ensure you stick to your program?

_____
_____
_____
_____

Off the top of your head, what are the biggest changes that you have made that have made the most impact?

Personal:

_____
_____
_____
_____
_____

Professional:

_____
_____
_____
_____
_____
_____
_____

WEEK 4 FLY PHASE

Family:

_____
_____
_____
_____
_____

Impact on others:

_____
_____
_____
_____
_____

Have your goals changed since starting week 1? If so, how?

_____
_____
_____
_____
_____

Restate and Redefine your top three strategic goals for the next 30 and 90 days below:

Next 30 Days:

_____
_____
_____
_____
_____

Next 90 Days:

_____
_____
_____
_____
_____

WEEK 4 FLY PHASE

What have been the biggest changes you have made to declutter your mind, your area, your routine to focus more on your priorities that align with your goals?

_____

_____

_____

_____

_____

What can you do to further your improvements now that the initial 30 day program is coming to an end.

_____

_____

_____

_____

_____

What changes have made the biggest difference in creating more flow and less drag with your activities to help you focus on the things that are most important to you?

_____

_____

_____

_____

_____

What can you do to further those changes to increase performance and mental health?

_____

_____

_____

_____

_____

_____

_____

_____

WEEK 4 FLY PHASE

What is something else not listed above you have identified within the last two weeks that has helped you, or is working for you now, that you were not doing before you started Week 1 of the program?

_____
_____
_____
_____

How does your performance relate to keeping your word and promises with yourself and others?

_____
_____
_____
_____

What are you doing to celebrate your wins? How can you enjoy your life and successes more while staying aligned with your goals?

_____
_____
_____
_____
_____

ON-DEMAND RELAXATION / ENERGY

What are the three biggest changes you have made to create life balance between being "on" in your go-mode at work, fitness, at home, etc. and your "off switch" being in relaxation mode?

_____
_____
_____
_____

WEEK 4 FLY PHASE

What routines, rituals, or habits are you practicing ensuring you maintain your balance? Answer this in all categories below.

Personal:

_____
_____
_____
_____
_____

Professional:

_____
_____
_____
_____

Family / Relationships:

_____
_____
_____
_____
_____

Impact on the world and others:

_____
_____
_____
_____
_____
_____
_____
_____

WEEK 4 FLY PHASE

What areas do you still see or feel resistance locking in these habits and going back to old patterns? Be honest with yourself.

_____
_____
_____
_____
_____

What areas have worked for you in breaking through resistance to get closer to your goals and what you want for yourself and others around you?

_____
_____
_____
_____

For repetition, list out below the changes needed to implement this week to create balance. If they are similar to last week make sure you re-define what they are and why they are important to you this week.

A. Three changes in your daily routine to add more balance related to on and off switch:

_____
_____
_____
_____

B. Three changes in your week to create more flow / less drag with your activities:

_____
_____
_____
_____

WEEK 4 FLY PHASE

How have you / are you changing your nutrition to align more with your goals?

_____
_____
_____
_____
_____

How has your nutrition changed since week 1?

_____
_____
_____
_____
_____

What will your nutrition look like in 90 days?

_____
_____
_____
_____
_____

How has your workout routine changed since starting Week 1? What is your focus or priorities of work this week? This month?

_____
_____
_____
_____
_____

What will it look like in 30 days? 90 days?

_____
_____
_____
_____
_____

WEEK 4 FLY PHASE

How have you increased your rest time, sleep, and meditation to declutter your mind and recover at a higher level? What is working best for you? What are you having the most resistance with?

_____

_____

_____

_____

_____

Are you still using the word "try" in pursuit of your goals? Example: I am going to try to be on my phone less, or try to go to sleep at a decent time or have you removed it?

_____

_____

_____

_____

How charged are you spiritually? What have you done that has elevated this for you in the last month?

_____

_____

_____

_____

_____

_____

What book are you reading now?

_____

_____

_____

_____

_____

_____

WEEK 4 FLY PHASE

What creative outlets empower you? How have your habits evolved in this area in the last month?

_____

_____

_____

_____

_____

What will your creative time look like in 30 days? 90 days?

_____

_____

_____

_____

_____

_____

How have you mixed up your training schedule to ensure that you are not getting stuck in the "law of accommodation" principle? Example, once your routine becomes routine or comfortable it stops being as effective.

_____

_____

_____

_____

_____

_____

What people, places, and activities have you changed this month to add more flow and less drag in your life?

_____

_____

_____

_____

_____

_____

_____

WEEK 4 FLY PHASE

What standards will you hold yourself too moving forward with the individuals and activities you surround yourself with?

_____
_____
_____
_____
_____
_____

How are you keeping yourself accountable with your goals? What people in your circle have you shared your progress, commitments, and goals with?

_____
_____
_____
_____
_____
_____

How will this continue moving forward?

_____
_____
_____
_____
_____

Lastly – A big trend with success in this program is keeping a journal. How can you / are you using a journal to stay accountable, creative, and consistent with yourself? This can be a notebook or dedicated notes app on your phone whatever works for you. Write in it daily to increase your effectiveness with the program.

_____
_____
_____
_____
_____

WEEK 4 FLY PHASE

When we write down and speak our goals it creates a positive energy that attaches to them. How can you increase the energy around the most important goals in your life?

_____
_____
_____
_____
_____

How are you celebrating your wins in these areas individually and with close people in your circle?

_____
_____
_____
_____
_____
_____

ECONOMY OF MOTION

What were the biggest realizations from the last month about your schedule that create drag for you in your daily flow and in your week? List the top three below.

Personal:

_____
_____
_____
_____
_____

Professional:

_____
_____
_____
_____
_____

WEEK 4 FLY PHASE

Family/Relationships:

_____
_____
_____
_____
_____

What changes have you made to increase the flow overall?

_____
_____
_____
_____
_____

How will you continue to assess your economy of motion and flow vs. drag moving forward?

_____
_____
_____
_____
_____

How can you strategically plan or make adjustments to your pattern of life (movement) throughout your day / week to make it flow even better? Remember, less is more.

_____
_____
_____
_____
_____
_____

WEEK 4 FLY PHASE

EFFICIENT BREATHING

What was your maximum breath you took in (in seconds) in Week 4?

_____

_____

_____

_____

_____

What is your maximum breath hold on land (in seconds)?

_____

_____

_____

_____

_____

What have you found out about your breathing over the last month in relation to your overall performance and how you manage stress?

_____

_____

_____

_____

_____

What are your breathing goals moving forward?

_____

_____

_____

_____

_____

_____

_____

_____

WEEK 4 WRAP-UP

"Law of Accommodation is the response of a biological object to a given constant stimulus decreased over time. Thus, accommodation is the decrease in response of your body to a constant continued stimulus. In training, the stimulus is physical exercise."

-Vladimir M. Zatsiorsky

We can learn a lot about ourselves in 30 days. What will your next 30 days look like? Take time to reflect on your last month and what areas you need to focus on or change to bring yourself closer to your goals moving forward. The biological law of accommodation (graphic below) reinforces the need to "mix things up" and change up workouts, nutrition, and recovery processes to continue to increase performance gains.

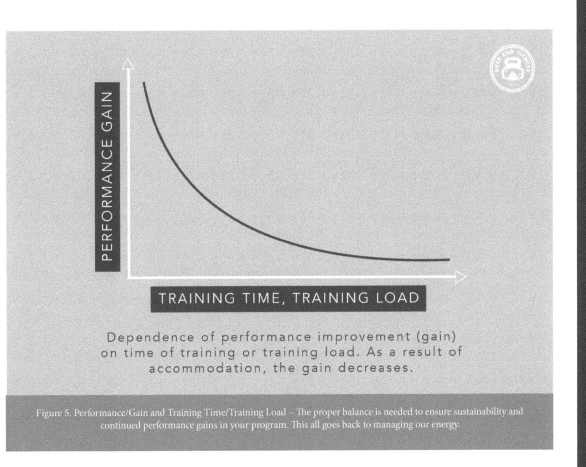

Dependence of performance improvement (gain) on time of training or training load. As a result of accommodation, the gain decreases.

Figure 5. Performance/Gain and Training Time/Training Load – The proper balance is needed to ensure sustainability and continued performance gains in your program. This all goes back to managing our energy.

WEEK 4 SELF-REFLECTION SCORES

On a scale of 1 - 10, rate how you showed up for yourself this week in each of these key attributes.

Effort:
1 2 3 4 5 6 7 8 9 10

Accountability:
1 2 3 4 5 6 7 8 9 10

Performance:
1 2 3 4 5 6 7 8 9 10

Self-Confidence:
1 2 3 4 5 6 7 8 9 10

Consistency:
1 2 3 4 5 6 7 8 9 10

Discipline:
1 2 3 4 5 6 7 8 9 10

"Calm in the Clutch":
1 2 3 4 5 6 7 8 9 10

Setting Boundaries:
1 2 3 4 5 6 7 8 9 10

Ability to Surrender:
1 2 3 4 5 6 7 8 9 10

Flow:
1 2 3 4 5 6 7 8 9 10

On a scale of 1 - 10, rate how you showed up for your people this week in each of these key attributes.

Family:
1 2 3 4 5 6 7 8 9 10

Friends:
1 2 3 4 5 6 7 8 9 10

Coworkers:
1 2 3 4 5 6 7 8 9 10

EXAMPLE 4 WEEK KEY ATTRIBUTES

Use the graph on the following page to chart your progress during these past four weeks. Below is an example and the list of key attributes you will be focusing on:

1. EFFORT 2. ACCOUNTABILITY 3. PERFORMANCE 4. SELF-CONFIDENCE
5. CONSISTENCY 6. DISCIPLINE 7. CALM IN CLUTCH 8. SETTING BOUNDARIES
9. SURRENDERING 10. FAMILY 11. FRIENDS 12. CO-WORKERS

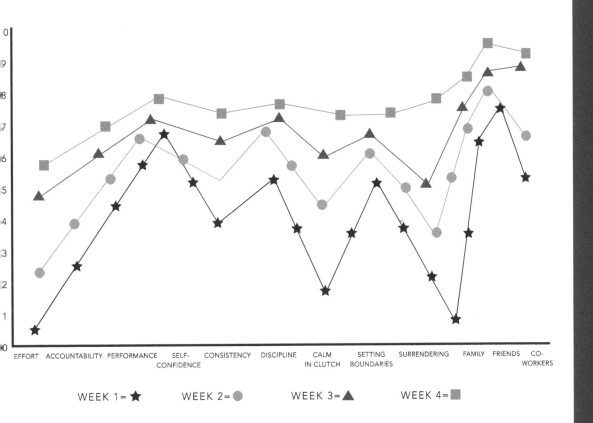

WEEK 1 = ★   WEEK 2 = ●   WEEK 3 = ▲   WEEK 4 = ■

4 WEEKS KEY ATTRIBUTES SUMMARY

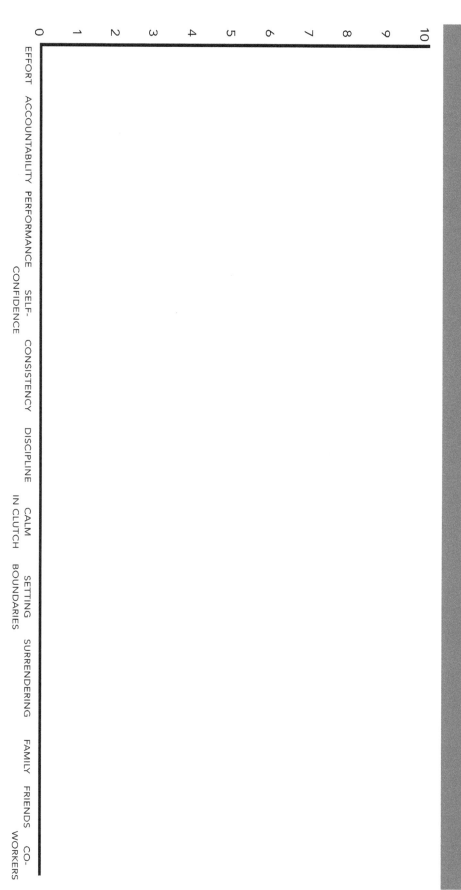

	10
	9
	8
	7
	6
	5
	4
	3
	2
	1
	0

EFFORT   ACCOUNTABILITY   PERFORMANCE   SELF-CONFIDENCE   CONSISTENCY   DISCIPLINE   CALM IN CLUTCH   SETTING BOUNDARIES   SURRENDERING   FAMILY   FRIENDS   CO-WORKERS

WEEK 1 = ★   WEEK 2 = ●   WEEK 3 = ▲   WEEK 4 = ■

FOLLOW UP

As we conclude these four weeks of self-reflection, begin building strong meaningful habits, and strengthening our relationships with our people, it is imperative that we continue what we have learned within ourselves. It's common to lose the gains we have made with our new resolutions quickly. This is because most people make the goals without really making a plan to carry it out. Throughout this workbook you have developed and have been able to maintain your mental gains and flow by actively doing the weekly reflections and checking in with your accountability coach. Now that you have finished the workbook, the flow and processes you have developed are up to you to maintain. It is important to create all of the follow-up steps as part of the process. This is something you can do quickly but meaningfully by:

Taking the Time to Plan Out and Adjust the Details: Remember the plan and environment is ever shifting, continue to adjust your plan to improve your economy of motion towards your current and future goals.

Date for Your Resolution: Have an end date in sight for each goal you have, include and new goals you develop in the future.

Work Toward Your Resolution on a Daily Basis: Regardless of the resolution that you make, it is important that you are constantly keeping it as a primary focus.

Take a Few Minutes Each Week to Evaluate Your Progress: Pick one day each week where you will check on your progress.

Ritualize, Ritualize, Ritualize: Make your habits healthy rituals and associate it with someone you love and care about. Who are you trying to be the best version of yourself for? Your family? Yourself?

ROAD TO SELF-ACTUALIZATION

We recognize self-actualization as a state of achievement for an individual or athlete that reaches a point where they unlock their full potential: creativity, acceptance of facts (surrender), contribution to others, morality (understanding of right and wrong), and problem solving. A lot of us can get stuck in "security mode" which is actually a fear mindset and would fall at the bottom of the triangle on Maslow's hierarchy of needs. Our goal is to be in an abundance mindset open to possibility and improvement.

Self-actualization represents a concept derived from psychological theory created by Abraham Maslow. Self-actualization, according to Maslow, represents growth of an individual toward fulfillment of the highest needs structured towards ones' meaning and purpose in life. He states that self-actualizing individuals are able to resolve differences and self-challenges in the dilemma of choice and acceptance. Self-actualized individuals are highly creative and able to assess an issue critically to evaluate multiple solutions and outcomes.

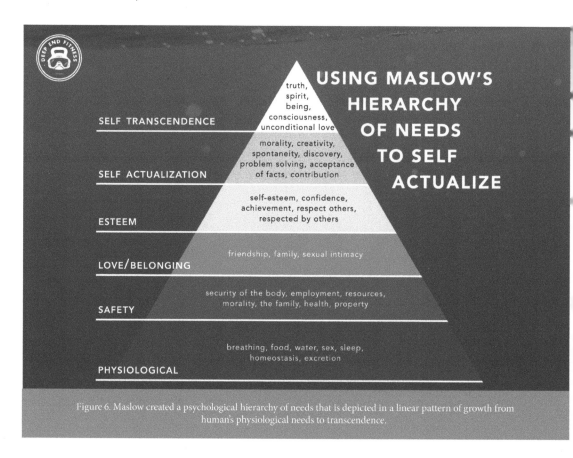

Figure 6. Maslow created a psychological hierarchy of needs that is depicted in a linear pattern of growth from human's physiological needs to transcendence.

ROAD TO SELF-ACTUALIZATION

MASLOW'S HIERARCHY IS AS FOLLOWS:

Physiological Needs: Breathing, food, sleep, water, etc.

Safety Needs: Need for security and protection, to include financial, social, and political.

Belonging and Love: Need of meaningful relationships, unselfish love that is based upon growth rather than deficiency.

Self-Esteem: Need for self love, self-respect, and healthy, positive feelings derived from confidence.

Self Actualization and Transcendence: Need for creative self-growth, fulfillment of potential and meaning in life.

With the things you have discovered about yourself in this workbook, where would you place yourself in this hierarchy? If you are not where you want to be, how do we use the tools that we now have in our box to work towards that goal? How do we lead others to achieve the same level of self? We must remember that what we have gained throughout the journey to reach your goals may or has exceeded the purpose of our goals themselves. It is the process of us developing new skills and habits to identify issues and work towards becoming the best version of ourselves. Understanding this drives us closer to self actualization and transcendence.

CONCLUSION

"It does not matter how slowly you go as long as you do not stop."
- Confucius

Some days you are going to feel like you are not moving forward, even though you are. When you experience mental gains by keeping your word to yourself and staying consistent, you are moving forward. Crawl, Walk, Run, Fly. Now that you have an understanding of your baseline and where you are in relation to your goals, your foundation is built. Your foundation consists of: an enhanced relationship with yourself and others, ability to identify and mitigate "drag" to create flow with a focus on self-actualization. The ways we do this are through:

1. Mental FOCUS to declutter and discipline your mind.

2. Managing your Energy and not your Time to create more RELAXATION.

3. Increased ECONOMY of MOTION in your activities to create flow.

4. EFFICIENT BREATHING practices and strategies.

Make sure you are celebrating your wins and giving yourself enough recovery week by week. Stay focused on your objectives and maintain accountability of your actions and performance. Remember the Law of Accommodation, continue your program or adjust as needed to continue to increase your performance.

For more F.R.E.E. YOUR MIND programs including individual performance training, executive and team training, or any other programs from Don and Prime, please visit our website https://deependfitness.com/online-programs

"Go Deep. Live Empowered."
- Motto of Deep End Fitness and the Underwater Torpedo League

COACHES

Prime Hall: Former Special Operations Marine Raider and Water Survival Instructor, USC EMBA, San Diego Sports Innovators). For several years, Prime has successfully used the techniques in this workbook to coach world class athletes, business executives, and military Special Operations candidates looking to perform at a higher level. The immediate result has been a powerful shift in their lives. Prime's goal is to facilitate lasting life changes for as many as possible that, in turn, will create a better society.

Don Tran: (Master Trainer -Co-Founder of DEF and UTL, Former Special Operations Marine Raider and Water Survival Instructor, Chapman University B.S. Business Administration, CFL1, CPT). Don has a passion for coaching, relentless training, and intensive preparation. Don applies his real-world experience as a small unit leader in the military and business entrepreneur to coach efficient movement and mental fortitude through the DEF and UTL Program. Don strives to help athletes and individuals overcome fears and break boundaries. He currently lives and works in the Los Angeles area.

GLOSSARY

ACCOUNTABILITY:

Accountability is accepting responsibility for one's words and actions. It can be with yourself and others. Accountability eliminates the time and effort you spend on unnecessary activities and other unproductive behavior. Accountability starts with you.

ANXIETIES:

Fears we are holding on to. False evidence appearing real. (Examples: Fear of failure. Fear of success.)

CONFIDENCE:

To be confident means feeling sure of your abilities and yourself. This doesn't mean being presumptuous, but confident in capabilities.

CONFIDENCE TARGETS:

A confidence target is a milestone set up on the path towards your goal that builds confidence and reinforces commitment in yourself and in the process.

CONSISTENCY:

This comes down to how accountable you are with yourself and your coach. How often and reliable are you able to commit to creating your best performance, health, and relationships.

DISCIPLINE / FLOW / SURRENDER:

Discipline in our routines and consistency are the staples to following through on meeting goals. The other key focal point is to be present, which calls for us to surrender to the moment and our fears to break through to a flow state.

DRAG:

Any person, place, or thing that is preventing us from reaching our max potential. We can also create drag for ourselves by participating in activities or spending energy on things that don't serve us or align with our goals and our family.

ECONOMY OF MOTION:

The concept of minimizing unnecessary movements to improve the effectiveness of effort whether it be through body movement during exercise or the pattern of life you carry throughout your day.

GLOSSARY

EFFICIENT BREATHING:

Taking proper, diaphragmatic, relaxed and rhythmic breaths at the right time for the right reasons.

EGOLESS COACHING:

As coaches, we lead with no ego, and are transparent and vulnerable along with the participants in an experiential learning and coaching environment.

EGOLESS TRAINING:

We challenge all of our athletes to train with an open mind and limited if no ego during our training sessions in order to promote the most growth.

FEAR AND SCARCITY MINDSET INTO ABUNDANCE:

We do not operate at full potential and possibility for ourselves and others when we are coming from a fear-based or scarcity mindset. One of the best ways to increase your performance immediately is to come from a place of love, heal and enhance your key relationships. Second is believing in yourself. Outline and solidify in your mind what is possible for you.

FLOW:

Flow is the in between boredom and panic / balance of challenge and skill.

FLOW STATE:

Being in the zone, the mental state in which a person performing an activity is fully immersed in a feeling of energized focus, full involvement, and enjoyment in the process of the activity.

GAP:

An unfilled void or space; a break in continuity to reaching our goals.

GLASS CEILINGS:

Negative programming from our past or self limiting beliefs that we have heard and started to believe. For example."I could never hold my breath for two minutes."

LAW OF LEAST EFFORT:

The Law of Least Effort is a spiritual law about life that Deepak Chopra describes as, "the principle of least action, of no resistance". This is the principle of harmony and love.

GLOSSARY

MENTAL FOCUS:

Focus is the ability to concentrate in the present and the task at hand. In order to fully maintain focus on one thing, you must inherently ignore distractions.

ON-DEMAND RELAXATION:

The ability to calm your nerves and mind at any given moment and/or stressful situations.

PERFORMANCE:

This program is 80% mental and 20% Physical. When you are assessing yourself and your patterns in this program, assess yourself mentaly and physically.

SACRIFICES:

Discomfort is going to be part of reaching your true potential. You are going to be stretched in your path to your own greatness. Your biggest breakdowns can lead to your biggest breakthroughs.

TAKE TIME TO SLOW DOWN - GET OUT OF REACTION MODE:

The world is viral around us. Oftentimes we can be in fight or flight mode and reaction mode (autopilot feeling like there is never enough time) that feeling in control of their environment. One way to slow down is to focus on breathing with your diaphragm in through your nose, out through your mouth for different variations. Example: 5 seconds in nose, Slow exhale 10 seconds through your mouth. Repeat 5 times.

TRYOUT:

We think of a tryout as a challenge. Are we challenging ourselves enough in our daily lives to create a flow state?